Table of Contents

Chapter 1: Introduction to Cross-Border Payments 3
    Understanding Cross-Border Payments 3
    The Challenges of Traditional Payment Systems 4
    The Role of Cryptocurrencies in Modern Finance 5

Chapter 2: Overview of Stellar Lumens 7
    What is Stellar Lumens? 8
    Key Features of the Stellar Network 9
    How Stellar Differs from Other Cryptocurrencies 11

Chapter 3: Mastering Cross-Border Payments with Stellar 12
    The Mechanics of Cross-Border Transactions 13
    Benefits of Using Stellar for Cross-Border Payments 14
    Real-World Use Cases and Success Stories 16

Chapter 4: Decentralized Finance (DeFi) Applications on Stellar 17
    Introduction to DeFi 18
    Stellar's DeFi Ecosystem 19
    Innovative DeFi Projects on Stellar 21

Chapter 5: Non-Fungible Tokens (NFTs) and Stellar 22
    Understanding NFTs 23
    How Stellar Facilitates NFT Creation 24
    Case Studies of NFTs on the Stellar Network 26

Chapter 6: Tokenization of Assets on the Stellar Network 27
    The Concept of Tokenization 28
    Benefits of Asset Tokenization 29
    Examples of Tokenized Assets on Stellar 31

Chapter 7: Smart Contracts and Automation in Stellar 32
    Introduction to Smart Contracts 33
    How Smart Contracts Work on Stellar 34
    Applications of Smart Contracts in Cross-Border Payments 36

Chapter 8: Stellar Network Security and Scalability 37
    Security Features of the Stellar Network 38
    Addressing Scalability Challenges 39
    Future Developments in Stellar Security and Scalability 40

Chapter 9: The Role of XLM in Philanthropy and Humanitarian Aid Projects 42
    Overview of Philanthropy in the Crypto Space 43
    Notable Humanitarian Projects Using XLM 44
    The Impact of Stellar on Global Philanthropy 46

Chapter 10: The Future of Cross-Border Payments with Stellar 47
    Trends Shaping the Future of Payments 48
    The Potential of Stellar in Global Financial Inclusion 49
    Predictions for the Next Decade in Cross-Border Payments 51

Copyright © 2024 by B.A. Blacksmith

All rights reserved.

No portion of this book may be reproduced in any form without written permission from the publisher or author, except as permitted by U.S. copyright law.

Chapter 1: Introduction to Cross-Border Payments

Understanding Cross-Border Payments

Understanding cross-border payments is essential for grasping the transformative potential of cryptocurrencies, particularly Stellar Lumens (XLM). Cross-border payments refer to transactions where funds are sent from one country to another, often involving multiple currencies and financial institutions. Traditional systems for these payments can be slow, costly, and prone to errors. The advent of digital currencies, especially XLM, offers a streamlined alternative that enhances speed, reduces fees, and increases accessibility for users worldwide.

Stellar Lumens is specifically designed to facilitate fast and low-cost cross-border transactions. By utilizing a decentralized network, Stellar enables users to send money directly to one another without the need for intermediaries like banks, which can significantly reduce transaction times from days to mere seconds. This efficiency is crucial for both individuals and businesses that rely on timely payments to maintain operations and relationships across borders. With Stellar's unique protocol, users can transact in various currencies, making it an ideal solution for international remittances and trade.

The integration of decentralized finance (DeFi) applications on the Stellar network further enhances its capabilities in cross-border payments. DeFi applications can provide additional financial services, such as lending, borrowing, and trading, without the need for traditional financial institutions. This democratization of financial services allows users from different parts of the world to access capital, manage their assets, and engage in cross-border trade more effectively. Stellar's infrastructure supports these applications, offering a secure and scalable environment for innovation in financial services.

In addition to facilitating payments, Stellar Lumens plays a significant role in the tokenization of assets and the creation of non-fungible tokens (NFTs). By enabling the representation of real-world assets on the blockchain, Stellar allows users to transfer ownership of property, art, and other valuable items seamlessly across borders. This capability not only opens up new markets for investors but also enhances liquidity for asset holders. The rise of NFTs on the Stellar network illustrates the potential for unique digital assets to be traded globally, further expanding the possibilities for cross-border transactions.

Lastly, the security and scalability of the Stellar network are pivotal in understanding its effectiveness in cross-border payments. Stellar employs advanced cryptographic techniques to ensure the security of transactions, making it a reliable choice for users concerned about the safety of their funds. Additionally, its ability to handle a large volume of transactions without compromising speed positions Stellar as a strong contender in the evolving landscape of digital currencies. As more individuals and organizations recognize the benefits of using XLM for cross-border payments, the network is poised to play a vital role in the future of global finance, including philanthropic efforts and humanitarian aid projects that require efficient and reliable funding mechanisms.

The Challenges of Traditional Payment Systems

Traditional payment systems face a myriad of challenges that can hinder efficiency and accessibility, particularly in the context of cross-border transactions. One of the primary issues is the high cost associated with international transfers. Banks and financial institutions often impose steep fees for processing these transactions, which can significantly reduce the amount received by the recipient. Additionally, currency conversion rates can vary widely, adding another layer of expense that can discourage individuals and businesses from engaging in cross-border economic activities.

Another challenge is the time it takes for traditional payment systems to process transactions. International wire transfers can take several days to complete, leading to frustration for both senders and recipients. This delay can be particularly problematic in urgent situations, such as humanitarian aid efforts where timely access to funds is crucial. The inefficiency of traditional systems often results in lost opportunities, especially for businesses that rely on quick transactions to maintain their operations and competitiveness in the global market.

Regulatory compliance is another significant hurdle for traditional payment systems. Financial institutions must navigate a complex web of regulations that can vary by country, creating barriers to seamless transactions. This complexity can result in additional delays and costs, as financial institutions may need to invest in compliance measures and legal consultations. For many small businesses and individuals, these regulatory burdens can be overwhelming, leading them to avoid international transactions altogether.

Security concerns also plague traditional payment systems. Cybersecurity threats, identity theft, and fraud are persistent risks that can compromise the safety of transactions. While banks and institutions implement various security measures, breaches still occur, leading to lost funds and eroded trust among users. The lack of transparency in these systems can exacerbate these concerns, as individuals may feel uncertain about the safety of their financial information and assets.

Finally, traditional payment systems often lack inclusivity. Many people around the world remain unbanked or underbanked, limiting their access to essential financial services. This exclusion is particularly evident in developing countries, where traditional banking infrastructure is limited or non-existent. As a result, individuals in these regions may struggle to engage in global commerce, hindering their economic potential. In contrast, innovative solutions like Stellar Lumens aim to address these challenges by providing a decentralized, efficient, and accessible platform for cross-border payments, empowering individuals and businesses alike.

The Role of Cryptocurrencies in Modern Finance

The emergence of cryptocurrencies has fundamentally shifted the landscape of modern finance, introducing new paradigms for transactions, investments, and financial systems. At the forefront of this change is Stellar Lumens (XLM), a digital currency designed specifically for facilitating cross-border payments. Cryptocurrencies like XLM are not only enhancing traditional financial services but are also enabling faster, cheaper, and more secure transactions across borders. This is particularly significant in an increasingly globalized economy where the need for efficient financial solutions is paramount.

One of the most notable roles of cryptocurrencies in modern finance is their ability to provide access to financial services for the unbanked and underbanked populations around the world. Stellar Lumens leverages blockchain technology to create a decentralized network that allows individuals to send money directly to one another without the need for intermediaries like banks. This capability is particularly advantageous in regions where traditional banking infrastructure is lacking, and it empowers individuals to participate in the global economy. By fostering financial inclusion, cryptocurrencies are reshaping the traditional financial landscape and providing opportunities for economic growth in underserved communities.

Decentralized finance (DeFi) applications built on the Stellar network further illustrate the transformative potential of cryptocurrencies in modern finance. DeFi platforms eliminate the need for central authorities, allowing users to lend, borrow, and trade assets directly with one another. This democratization of finance not only enhances transparency but also reduces costs associated with traditional financial services. Stellar's smart contract capabilities enable automated processes that execute transactions based on predefined conditions, making financial transactions more efficient. By integrating DeFi solutions, Stellar Lumens is positioning itself as a key player in the evolution of financial systems.

Non-fungible tokens (NFTs) and the tokenization of assets on the Stellar network represent another significant development in the role of cryptocurrencies. NFTs allow for the ownership and transfer of unique digital assets, while tokenization enables real-world assets, such as real estate or art, to be represented on the blockchain. This innovation promotes liquidity and fractional ownership, making it easier for individuals to invest in high-value assets. With Stellar's low transaction costs and fast processing times, these applications can be executed seamlessly, opening new avenues for investment and asset management.

Lastly, the security and scalability of the Stellar network play a crucial role in its adoption as a viable financial solution. Stellar's consensus mechanism ensures that transactions are secure and validated quickly, which is essential for maintaining trust in digital currencies. As the demand for cryptocurrencies continues to grow, Stellar's ability to scale efficiently positions it well for future developments in finance. Furthermore, the application of XLM in philanthropy and humanitarian aid projects showcases the potential of cryptocurrencies to address global challenges, enabling faster and more transparent donations and funding distributions. Overall, the integration of cryptocurrencies into modern finance heralds a new era of opportunities for investors and individuals alike, particularly through the versatile capabilities of Stellar Lumens.

Chapter 2: Overview of Stellar Lumens

What is Stellar Lumens?

Stellar Lumens, often abbreviated as XLM, is the native cryptocurrency of the Stellar network, a decentralized platform designed to facilitate cross-border payments and the transfer of assets with remarkable speed and minimal cost. Stellar was founded by Jed McCaleb in 2014, aiming to bridge the gap between traditional financial systems and the burgeoning world of digital currencies. By leveraging blockchain technology, Stellar provides a secure, efficient, and inclusive framework for transferring value across borders, making it an ideal solution for those seeking to overcome the limitations of conventional banking methods.

The Stellar network operates on a unique consensus protocol known as the Stellar Consensus Protocol (SCP), which allows transactions to be confirmed quickly and securely. This system eliminates the need for mining, making it energy-efficient and enhancing its scalability. Stellar's design allows for the integration of various assets, including fiat currencies, cryptocurrencies, and even commodities, enabling users to send and receive payments in multiple forms. This flexibility makes Stellar particularly appealing for cross-border transactions, where currency conversion and transfer fees can be significant barriers.

One of the standout features of Stellar Lumens is its capacity to support decentralized finance (DeFi) applications. Through smart contracts and automated processes, developers can create a variety of financial products and services on the Stellar network. This capability not only democratizes access to financial services but also fosters innovation within the cryptocurrency space. The Stellar network's low transaction fees and fast processing times further enhance the viability of DeFi applications, allowing users to engage in lending, borrowing, and trading with ease.

In addition to its financial applications, Stellar is also making strides in the world of non-fungible tokens (NFTs) and asset tokenization. The network's infrastructure supports the creation and exchange of NFTs, enabling artists and creators to monetize their work in new ways. Furthermore, Stellar's asset tokenization capabilities allow real-world assets, such as real estate or art, to be represented on the blockchain, promoting liquidity and accessibility. This functionality is particularly useful for investors and collectors, as it opens up new avenues for diversification and investment.

Stellar Lumens is not only focused on finance and technology but also has a significant impact on philanthropy and humanitarian aid. The network has been utilized in various projects aimed at providing financial services to underserved populations and facilitating international remittances at a fraction of traditional costs. By enabling direct transfers to those in need, Stellar addresses critical issues such as poverty and financial exclusion, showcasing the potential of blockchain technology to drive positive social change. As interest in Stellar Lumens continues to grow, its multifaceted applications reinforce its position as a vital player in the evolving landscape of cryptocurrencies and blockchain solutions.

Key Features of the Stellar Network

The Stellar Network is designed to facilitate fast, low-cost cross-border transactions, making it a powerful tool for individuals and businesses alike. One of its key features is its ability to process transactions in just a few seconds, regardless of geographical barriers. This speed is crucial in the world of finance, where time-sensitive transactions are common. The Stellar Consensus Protocol (SCP) underpins this rapid processing capability, allowing nodes in the network to reach consensus quickly without the need for extensive computational power. This efficiency not only enhances user experience but also lowers transaction costs, making Stellar particularly attractive for remittances and international payments.

Another significant aspect of the Stellar Network is its focus on financial inclusivity. By enabling individuals in underserved regions to access financial services, Stellar aims to bridge the gap between traditional banking systems and the unbanked population. Users can create a Stellar wallet and start transacting with minimal barriers, such as high fees or complicated verification processes. This democratization of finance supports a wide array of applications, including microloans and peer-to-peer transactions, which can empower individuals and communities economically.

The Stellar Network also supports the creation and exchange of various digital assets, including stablecoins and tokens representing real-world assets. This tokenization capability opens up innovative avenues for investment and asset management. Investors can leverage Stellar to create custom tokens that represent ownership of assets ranging from real estate to art. These tokens can then be traded seamlessly on the Stellar Network, providing liquidity and accessibility that traditional asset markets often lack. This feature is particularly beneficial for DeFi applications, where users can participate in lending, borrowing, and yield farming using tokenized assets.

Furthermore, the implementation of smart contracts on the Stellar Network adds a layer of automation and efficiency to transactions. Smart contracts enable developers to automate processes, reducing the need for intermediaries and minimizing the potential for human error. This capability enhances transparency and trust within the network, as all parties can verify the terms of the contract and the execution of transactions in real time. The combination of smart contracts and Stellar's fast transaction speeds creates a robust environment for developing decentralized applications that cater to various use cases, including NFTs and automated financial services.

Lastly, security and scalability are pivotal features of the Stellar Network. The decentralized nature of the network, combined with its consensus mechanism, ensures that it is resistant to attacks and manipulation. This security is essential for users who want to engage in cross-border payments and other financial transactions without the fear of losing their assets. Additionally, Stellar's architecture is designed to scale efficiently as the network grows, accommodating an increasing number of transactions without sacrificing performance. This scalability positions Stellar as a viable contender in the blockchain space, particularly for projects focused on philanthropy and humanitarian aid, where the ability to transfer funds quickly and securely can have a profound impact on communities in need.

How Stellar Differs from Other Cryptocurrencies

Stellar stands out in the cryptocurrency landscape due to its unique focus on facilitating cross-border payments. Unlike many cryptocurrencies that prioritize speculative trading or operating as digital currencies, Stellar was specifically designed to enhance financial inclusion by enabling fast and cost-effective transactions across borders. Its primary goal is to connect financial institutions and drastically reduce transaction costs, which positions it as a vital tool for remittances and international trade. Stellar's consensus mechanism allows for faster transaction times compared to Bitcoin and Ethereum, making it particularly suitable for the needs of businesses and individuals engaged in global commerce.

Another distinctive feature of Stellar is its built-in decentralized exchange, which allows users to trade assets directly on the network. This functionality empowers users to convert one currency into another with minimal fees and without relying on centralized exchanges. While other cryptocurrencies may offer similar capabilities, Stellar's approach integrates this feature seamlessly into its network, thus enhancing liquidity and accessibility. This decentralized exchange model supports not just traditional currencies but also facilitates tokenization, allowing issuers to create new digital assets that can represent anything from real estate to art, thus broadening the scope of financial instruments available within the Stellar ecosystem.

Stellar also differentiates itself through its robust focus on security and scalability. The Stellar Consensus Protocol (SCP) enhances the network's resilience against attacks and ensures that transactions are processed efficiently. This is crucial for institutions that require a reliable network for their operations. In contrast, many cryptocurrencies face challenges related to scalability, often leading to congestion and high transaction costs during peak usage times. Stellar's design allows it to scale effectively, thereby supporting a growing number of transactions without compromising performance. This makes it an attractive option for enterprises looking to integrate blockchain technology into their operations.

In the realm of decentralized finance (DeFi) applications, Stellar offers unique advantages. While DeFi on other platforms may often grapple with issues of high fees and slow transaction speeds, Stellar's efficient architecture provides a more accessible environment for developers and users alike. As the DeFi sector continues to expand, Stellar's ability to support smart contracts and automate processes will likely play a significant role in shaping its evolution. This capability allows for the creation of innovative financial products and services, which can be tailored to meet the needs of diverse markets, particularly in regions where traditional banking services are lacking.

Finally, Stellar's commitment to philanthropy and humanitarian aid further sets it apart from other cryptocurrencies. The Stellar Development Foundation actively works to leverage the network for social good, emphasizing projects that aim to improve financial access and security for underserved populations. By facilitating low-cost remittances and fostering financial literacy through education, Stellar aims to create a more inclusive financial ecosystem. This focus on social impact resonates with investors and users who are increasingly looking for ways to align their financial activities with their values, making Stellar a compelling choice for those interested in harnessing the power of blockchain for positive change.

Chapter 3: Mastering Cross-Border Payments with Stellar

The Mechanics of Cross-Border Transactions

The mechanics of cross-border transactions within the context of Stellar Lumens (XLM) rely on a combination of advanced blockchain technology and the unique features of the Stellar network. At its core, the Stellar network functions as a decentralized platform that facilitates rapid and cost-efficient transfers of digital assets across borders. By utilizing the Stellar Consensus Protocol, transactions can be validated quickly and securely without the need for traditional intermediaries, such as banks, which often introduce delays and additional fees. This streamlining of processes is particularly beneficial for remittance services, allowing individuals to send money to family and friends in different countries with minimal costs.

One of the key components that enhance cross-border transactions on the Stellar network is the use of anchors. Anchors act as trusted intermediaries that hold deposits in various fiat currencies and issue corresponding tokens on the Stellar network. These tokens represent the fiat currency and can be transferred instantly between users. When a transaction occurs, the tokens are exchanged seamlessly, allowing for the quick conversion of one currency to another. This mechanism not only reduces the need for multiple currency exchanges but also provides users with a clear understanding of transaction values, helping to eliminate the uncertainties often associated with cross-border payments.

Moreover, Stellar's built-in decentralized exchange (DEX) allows users to trade assets directly on the network. This feature is crucial for cross-border transactions, as it enables users to convert currencies in real-time based on market rates, further enhancing the efficiency of the payment process. By leveraging the DEX, users can execute trades with reduced slippage and improved transparency, ensuring they get the best possible rates for their transactions. This decentralized approach mitigates the risks associated with centralized exchanges, such as security breaches and operational inefficiencies, making it a preferred choice for cross-border payments.

The integration of smart contracts on the Stellar network also plays a significant role in automating cross-border transactions. Smart contracts can be programmed to execute specific conditions automatically when predefined criteria are met, allowing for greater efficiency in managing complex transaction scenarios. For instance, in scenarios involving multiple parties or contingent payments, smart contracts can ensure that funds are only released when all parties have fulfilled their obligations. This automation reduces the need for manual intervention, minimizes the risk of errors, and accelerates the overall transaction process, making it an ideal solution for businesses engaging in international trade.

Lastly, security and scalability are paramount in the mechanics of cross-border transactions on Stellar. The network employs cryptographic techniques to ensure the integrity of transactions, protecting users from fraud and unauthorized access. Furthermore, Stellar's architecture is designed to handle a high volume of transactions, making it scalable for growing user demands. This scalability is crucial as more businesses and individuals turn to cryptocurrencies for cross-border payments, particularly in humanitarian aid projects where timely and secure transactions can significantly impact the delivery of assistance. By addressing these mechanics, Stellar Lumens positions itself as a robust solution for the future of cross-border payments, enabling seamless and efficient transactions on a global scale.

Benefits of Using Stellar for Cross-Border Payments

The use of Stellar for cross-border payments presents a transformative approach to international transactions, primarily due to its speed and cost-effectiveness. Traditional banking systems often involve multiple intermediaries, resulting in lengthy processing times and high fees. In contrast, Stellar's blockchain technology enables direct transactions between parties, significantly reducing both time and costs associated with cross-border payments. This efficiency is particularly beneficial for individuals and businesses that rely on swift financial interactions across different currencies and jurisdictions.

Another key advantage of utilizing Stellar for cross-border payments is its capability to handle multiple currencies seamlessly. Stellar's built-in decentralized exchange allows users to convert currencies in real-time, making it easier to transact in various fiat currencies or cryptocurrencies without the need for extensive currency conversion processes. This feature not only simplifies the user experience but also ensures that individuals and businesses can transact in their preferred currency, fostering greater accessibility and convenience in global commerce.

Stellar's focus on financial inclusion further enhances its appeal for cross-border payments. With over two billion people globally lacking access to traditional banking services, Stellar provides a viable alternative that empowers individuals in underserved regions. By enabling low-cost, fast transactions, Stellar opens up opportunities for those who previously faced barriers to financial participation. This makes it an attractive option for humanitarian aid organizations and philanthropic initiatives aiming to deliver financial assistance to communities in need, effectively boosting economic activity in those areas.

Security and transparency are also pivotal benefits of using Stellar for cross-border payments. The Stellar network employs advanced cryptographic techniques to secure transactions, ensuring that funds are protected against fraud and unauthorized access. Additionally, the transparency of the blockchain allows for real-time tracking of transactions, which can enhance trust among users. This level of security is crucial for businesses and investors who prioritize safe transactions, particularly in the increasingly digital landscape of finance.

Lastly, Stellar's scalability positions it as a formidable player in the cross-border payments space. As the demand for efficient cross-border transactions continues to grow, Stellar's architecture is designed to handle high transaction volumes without compromising performance. This scalability makes it suitable for both individual users and larger enterprises, enabling them to execute numerous transactions simultaneously without delays. As more businesses and individuals recognize the potential of Stellar, its role in reshaping the landscape of cross-border payments will continue to expand, driving innovation in the financial sector.

Real-World Use Cases and Success Stories

Real-world use cases of Stellar Lumens (XLM) illustrate its transformative potential in cross-border payments and beyond. One notable example is the partnership between Stellar and various financial institutions to streamline remittances. In countries with high emigration rates, such as the Philippines and Mexico, sending money back home can incur hefty fees and take several days. By utilizing Stellar's blockchain technology, these transactions can be processed in a matter of seconds at a fraction of the traditional cost, significantly benefiting both senders and recipients.

In the realm of decentralized finance (DeFi), Stellar has made strides by facilitating the creation of decentralized applications that enhance financial inclusion. Projects like StellarTerm enable users to trade assets without relying on centralized exchanges. This democratization of finance empowers individuals in underbanked regions to access financial services previously unavailable to them. The ability to swap tokens seamlessly on the Stellar network illustrates how DeFi can enhance liquidity and provide new investment opportunities for users globally.

Non-fungible tokens (NFTs) have also found their place on the Stellar network, showcasing its versatility. Artists and creators can mint NFTs representing their work, ensuring provenance and ownership on a decentralized ledger. The Stellar network's low transaction fees and fast processing times make it an attractive platform for artists looking to enter the NFT space without the high costs associated with other blockchains. This has led to an increase in digital art sales and engagement, further expanding the use of XLM within creative industries.

Tokenization of assets is another significant application of Stellar Lumens. Real estate, commodities, and even intellectual property can be tokenized, allowing for fractional ownership and easier transfer between parties. This innovation can unlock liquidity in traditionally illiquid markets, making it easier for investors to diversify their portfolios. By leveraging Stellar's smart contracts, transactions can be automated and executed based on predefined conditions, enhancing efficiency in asset management and trading.

Lastly, the use of Stellar in philanthropic and humanitarian aid projects highlights its capacity for social good. Organizations like the United Nations and various NGOs are exploring how Stellar can facilitate quicker and more transparent distribution of aid. By utilizing XLM for cross-border donations and remittances, these organizations can minimize the overhead costs associated with traditional financial channels, ensuring that more funds reach those in need. This application of Stellar technology not only showcases its scalability and security but also emphasizes the potential for cryptocurrencies to drive positive change in the world.

Chapter 4: Decentralized Finance (DeFi) Applications on Stellar

Introduction to DeFi

Decentralized Finance, commonly referred to as DeFi, represents a paradigm shift in the financial landscape, leveraging blockchain technology to create an open and permissionless financial system. Unlike traditional finance, which relies on intermediaries such as banks and financial institutions, DeFi utilizes smart contracts to facilitate transactions directly between parties. This innovation not only enhances accessibility to financial services but also reduces costs and increases transparency in financial operations. As the world increasingly embraces digital assets, understanding DeFi becomes crucial for those interested in cryptocurrencies and their applications.

The Stellar network, known for its speed and efficiency in cross-border payments, plays a pivotal role in the DeFi ecosystem. By enabling seamless transactions across borders with minimal fees, Stellar is uniquely positioned to support various DeFi applications. These applications range from lending platforms to decentralized exchanges, offering users the ability to interact with their assets in new and innovative ways. The integration of DeFi within the Stellar framework allows for a more inclusive financial system, where users can access services previously limited to those with traditional banking relationships.

In addition to facilitating cross-border payments, Stellar also supports the tokenization of assets, a key feature of the DeFi landscape. Tokenization allows real-world assets, such as real estate or art, to be represented digitally on the blockchain, enabling fractional ownership and greater liquidity. This process not only democratizes access to investment opportunities but also enhances transparency and security. By leveraging Stellar's capabilities, investors can engage in asset trading in a decentralized manner, reducing reliance on traditional financial structures.

Smart contracts, another essential component of DeFi, automate processes and ensure trustless transactions. On the Stellar network, smart contracts can be employed to execute trades, manage loans, and facilitate complex financial agreements without the need for intermediaries. This automation reduces the risk of human error and enhances the efficiency of financial transactions. Consequently, individuals and businesses can engage in financial activities with greater confidence, knowing that the terms of their agreements will be executed as intended.

As DeFi continues to evolve, it also presents opportunities for philanthropic initiatives and humanitarian aid projects. The transparency and low-cost nature of transactions on the Stellar network can significantly enhance the effectiveness of charitable donations and aid distribution. By utilizing DeFi applications, organizations can ensure that funds reach their intended recipients swiftly and without excessive fees. This intersection of DeFi and humanitarian efforts exemplifies the potential of blockchain technology to not only transform finance but also create a more equitable and just global economy.

Stellar's DeFi Ecosystem

Stellar's DeFi ecosystem is rapidly evolving, providing a robust framework for decentralized finance applications that enhance cross-border payment capabilities. With the growing demand for innovative financial solutions, Stellar Lumens (XLM) positions itself as a pivotal player in the DeFi space. The platform's unique architecture allows for seamless integration of various financial instruments, thereby enabling users to access a wide range of services, from lending and borrowing to yield farming and liquidity provision. By leveraging Stellar's fast transaction speeds and low fees, developers can create applications that cater to diverse financial needs while ensuring accessibility for users around the globe.

One of the most significant advantages of Stellar's DeFi ecosystem is its focus on tokenization. The Stellar network allows users to create and manage digital tokens representing real-world assets, such as currencies, commodities, or even NFTs. This capability facilitates the tokenization of a wide array of assets, enabling users to trade or leverage these tokens within the DeFi landscape. By providing a simple and efficient way to tokenize assets, Stellar empowers individuals and businesses to unlock liquidity and enhance their financial portfolios. This tokenization is especially beneficial in cross-border transactions, where traditional systems often struggle with inefficiencies and high costs.

Smart contracts and automation play crucial roles in Stellar's DeFi framework. Through the implementation of smart contracts, developers can automate various processes, reducing the need for intermediaries and increasing the efficiency of transactions. This automation not only streamlines processes such as trade execution and settlement but also enhances transparency and security. Additionally, the use of smart contracts allows for the creation of complex financial products tailored to specific user needs, further expanding the capabilities of the Stellar network in the DeFi space.

Security and scalability are other critical components of Stellar's DeFi ecosystem. The Stellar network employs a federated Byzantine agreement consensus mechanism, which ensures that transactions are secure and that the network can handle a high volume of transactions without compromising performance. This scalability is essential as the DeFi space continues to grow and attract more users. By maintaining a secure and scalable environment, Stellar provides a reliable foundation for developers to build innovative financial applications that can cater to both individual and institutional investors.

Finally, Stellar's DeFi ecosystem has significant implications for philanthropy and humanitarian aid projects. By enabling fast, low-cost transactions across borders, Stellar allows organizations to efficiently transfer funds to areas in need, facilitating quicker responses to crises. The platform's capabilities in tokenization and smart contracts can also be utilized to create transparent donation processes, ensuring that funds are allocated effectively and reach the intended recipients. As more organizations recognize the potential of Stellar in addressing global challenges, the intersection of DeFi and philanthropy will continue to grow, demonstrating the transformative power of decentralized finance in creating a more equitable financial landscape.

Innovative DeFi Projects on Stellar

Innovative DeFi projects on the Stellar network are transforming the landscape of decentralized finance by leveraging the unique capabilities of Stellar Lumens (XLM). As a blockchain designed for cross-border transactions, Stellar offers a high-speed, low-cost platform that attracts various DeFi applications. These projects aim to democratize access to financial services, allowing individuals and businesses, particularly in underbanked regions, to participate in global financial ecosystems. By utilizing Stellar's infrastructure, these projects are not only improving transaction efficiency but also introducing new financial products and services tailored to diverse user needs.

One notable project is StellarTerm, a decentralized exchange that enables users to trade digital assets directly on the Stellar network. With its user-friendly interface, StellarTerm allows individuals to swap different tokens, including stablecoins and other cryptocurrencies, without the need for a centralized intermediary. This feature enhances liquidity and opens up trading opportunities for users who may not have access to traditional exchanges. Additionally, StellarTerm's integration with Stellar's built-in asset issuance capabilities allows for seamless trading of new tokens that are created on the network, fostering innovation and growth within the Stellar ecosystem.

Another significant DeFi initiative is the development of automated market makers (AMMs) on Stellar. These platforms allow users to provide liquidity by depositing assets into pools, earning fees from trades executed within those pools. AMMs eliminate the need for order books and traditional trading mechanisms, facilitating quicker transactions and reducing slippage. By enabling users to earn passive income through liquidity provision, Stellar's AMMs are attracting liquidity from various sources, further enhancing the network's usability and appeal for investors seeking to diversify their portfolios.

Tokenization of assets is also gaining traction within the Stellar network, as innovative projects explore the possibilities of representing real-world assets on the blockchain. This includes everything from real estate to commodities, allowing for fractional ownership and improved liquidity. By tokenizing assets, Stellar enables more people to invest in high-value items that were traditionally out of reach, democratizing access to wealth-building opportunities. This capability not only enhances financial inclusion but also streamlines the process of buying, selling, and trading assets, making it more efficient and transparent.

Lastly, the integration of smart contracts within Stellar's DeFi projects is paving the way for automated and trustless transactions. These self-executing contracts facilitate various financial agreements without the need for intermediaries, reducing costs and increasing transaction speed. Projects utilizing smart contracts on Stellar can create innovative solutions for lending, insurance, and other financial services, further expanding the DeFi landscape. As these projects continue to evolve, they are likely to play a crucial role in shaping the future of finance, particularly in regions where traditional banking infrastructure is lacking.

Chapter 5: Non-Fungible Tokens (NFTs) and Stellar

Understanding NFTs

Non-fungible tokens, or NFTs, have emerged as a revolutionary concept within the blockchain landscape, capturing the interest of artists, collectors, and investors alike. Unlike cryptocurrencies such as Bitcoin or Stellar Lumens (XLM), which are fungible and can be exchanged on a one-to-one basis, NFTs are unique digital assets that represent ownership of specific items or content. This uniqueness grants NFTs their value, as each token contains distinct information that differentiates it from others. The applications of NFTs span various domains, including art, music, gaming, and even real estate, making them a versatile tool in the digital economy.

Within the Stellar Network, NFTs present an exciting opportunity for creators and investors, particularly in the realm of cross-border transactions. Stellar's infrastructure is designed for fast and cost-effective transfers, offering an ideal platform for minting and trading NFTs. Artists and content creators can leverage Stellar's capabilities to reach global audiences without the constraints posed by traditional financial systems. This democratization of access enables creators from diverse backgrounds to gain visibility and monetization opportunities for their work, fostering a vibrant ecosystem where creativity can thrive.

The tokenization of assets through NFTs also aligns with the principles of decentralized finance (DeFi) applications on Stellar. By representing physical or digital assets as NFTs, individuals can unlock new forms of liquidity and investment opportunities. For instance, a piece of real estate can be tokenized as an NFT, allowing multiple investors to own fractions of the property, thus lowering the barrier to entry for investment. This innovative approach promotes inclusivity in investment while simultaneously enhancing transparency and security, as all transactions are recorded on the blockchain.

Smart contracts play a crucial role in the functionality of NFTs on the Stellar Network. These self-executing contracts automate various processes, such as royalties for artists when their NFTs are sold or resold. By integrating smart contracts with NFTs, creators can ensure that they receive fair compensation for their work, even in secondary markets. This automation not only enhances the efficiency of transactions but also provides an additional layer of trust, as the terms of the agreement are enforced by the code itself rather than relying on intermediaries.

As the popularity of NFTs continues to grow, so does the need for security and scalability within the Stellar Network. The ability to handle a high volume of transactions while maintaining robust security measures is pivotal for fostering confidence among users. Stellar's design emphasizes scalability, ensuring that the network can accommodate the increasing demand for NFT transactions without compromising performance. Additionally, the decentralized nature of the Stellar Network mitigates risks associated with single points of failure, making it a reliable environment for the burgeoning NFT market. As stakeholders in the cryptocurrency space navigate the evolving landscape, understanding the nuances of NFTs will be essential for harnessing their potential within cross-border payments and beyond.

How Stellar Facilitates NFT Creation

The Stellar network provides a robust framework for the creation and management of non-fungible tokens (NFTs), which represent unique digital assets on the blockchain. Unlike traditional tokens that are interchangeable, NFTs possess distinct characteristics, making them ideal for representing ownership of digital art, collectibles, and various other assets. Stellar's architecture, designed for speed and efficiency, allows creators to mint NFTs without the high fees and slow transaction times often associated with other blockchain platforms. This accessibility is particularly beneficial for artists and creators looking to enter the burgeoning NFT market.

One of the key features of Stellar that facilitates NFT creation is its built-in tokenization capabilities. Users can create custom tokens with specific attributes tailored to their needs. This functionality allows for the representation of not just digital art, but also real-world assets, such as real estate or intellectual property, thus broadening the scope of what can be tokenized. The simplicity of the Stellar Development Foundation's tools and APIs encourages developers to innovate and create unique NFT projects that can cater to various niches within the market.

Stellar also prioritizes scalability and security, essential elements for any platform handling digital assets. The Stellar Consensus Protocol enables fast transaction processing, which is crucial for NFT marketplaces that require quick confirmation times for buying and selling. Additionally, Stellar's focus on security through decentralized validation mechanisms ensures that NFT ownership and transactions are transparent and tamper-proof. This level of security builds trust among users, which is vital in the increasingly competitive NFT space.

Another significant advantage of using Stellar for NFTs is its integration with decentralized finance (DeFi) applications. Creators can leverage DeFi tools to enhance the utility of their NFTs, such as using them as collateral for loans or integrating them into liquidity pools. This interoperability between NFTs and DeFi on the Stellar network opens up new avenues for monetization and engagement, allowing creators to earn passive income while providing additional value to their audiences.

Finally, Stellar's commitment to social impact through initiatives in philanthropy and humanitarian aid demonstrates its potential beyond mere asset creation. NFTs can be utilized to raise funds for charitable causes, with proceeds going directly to organizations that support various humanitarian efforts. This aspect of NFT creation aligns with the growing trend of purposeful investing, where investors seek to support projects that contribute positively to society. By facilitating NFT creation in a way that emphasizes both innovation and social good, Stellar positions itself as a leader in the evolving landscape of digital assets.

Case Studies of NFTs on the Stellar Network

Case studies of NFTs on the Stellar Network illustrate the versatility and potential of this blockchain technology in the digital asset space. Stellar's unique architecture, designed for cross-border transactions and low-cost operations, provides an ideal foundation for the creation and trading of non-fungible tokens. Unlike other networks that may face congestion and high fees, Stellar allows for seamless interactions, making it appealing for artists, creators, and investors looking to engage in the NFT market.

One notable case is the collaboration between Stellar and various artists to issue limited-edition digital art as NFTs. This initiative not only empowers creators by providing them with direct access to global markets but also ensures that transaction fees remain minimal, allowing artists to retain a larger portion of their earnings. The ability to tokenize art on the Stellar Network facilitates provenance and authenticity, addressing common concerns in the art world regarding forgery and ownership. Artists can embed smart contracts into their NFTs to automate royalties, ensuring they receive ongoing compensation as their work is resold.

Another significant example involves the use of NFTs for tokenizing real estate assets on the Stellar Network. By representing property ownership as NFTs, this approach simplifies the buying, selling, and leasing of real estate, particularly in cross-border transactions. Investors can purchase fractional ownership in properties, increasing accessibility to real estate investment. The efficiency and transparency of the Stellar blockchain enhance trust among stakeholders, as every transaction is recorded immutably, reducing disputes and streamlining due diligence processes.

In the realm of gaming, Stellar has been leveraged to create unique in-game assets as NFTs. This application demonstrates how digital collectibles can be traded and owned on a decentralized platform, fostering a vibrant economy within gaming communities. Players benefit from true ownership of their in-game items, which can be bought, sold, or traded across different games and platforms. The low fees associated with transactions on the Stellar Network encourage microtransactions, allowing for a more dynamic and engaging gaming experience.

Lastly, the integration of NFTs in philanthropy showcases the broader social impact of the Stellar Network. Nonprofits can create NFTs representing charitable contributions or awareness campaigns, allowing supporters to own a piece of the initiative. This approach not only raises funds but also creates a sense of community among donors. By utilizing Stellar's efficient payment system, charities can ensure that a greater percentage of donations goes directly to their causes, enhancing the overall effectiveness of humanitarian efforts. Through these case studies, it is evident that the Stellar Network is not only a facilitator of cross-border payments but also a transformative platform for the NFT ecosystem.

Chapter 6: Tokenization of Assets on the Stellar Network

The Concept of Tokenization

The concept of tokenization refers to the process of converting rights to an asset into a digital token that can be managed and transferred on a blockchain network. In the context of Stellar Lumens, tokenization allows a wide variety of assets to be represented as tokens on the Stellar blockchain, facilitating their exchange and interaction within the ecosystem. This process can include anything from traditional financial assets like stocks and bonds to real estate, art, and even intellectual property. By digitizing assets, tokenization enhances liquidity, increases market accessibility, and simplifies the transfer process, which is particularly vital for cross-border transactions.

One of the primary advantages of tokenization on the Stellar network is its ability to reduce friction in cross-border payments. Traditional methods often involve multiple intermediaries, leading to delays and increased costs. By tokenizing assets and utilizing Stellar's fast, low-cost transaction capabilities, individuals and businesses can transfer value seamlessly across borders. This efficiency opens up new avenues for international trade and can greatly benefit those in developing nations who may not have access to conventional banking infrastructure.

Tokenization also plays a significant role in decentralized finance (DeFi) applications built on the Stellar network. By representing assets as tokens, users can leverage them in smart contracts, enabling complex financial transactions without the need for intermediaries. This aspect not only enhances the speed of transactions but also democratizes financial services by allowing anyone with internet access to participate in the global economy. As DeFi continues to grow, the importance of tokenized assets will become increasingly pronounced, particularly in providing liquidity and diverse investment opportunities.

Non-fungible tokens (NFTs) are another exciting application of tokenization on the Stellar network. Unlike standard cryptocurrencies, NFTs represent unique assets, making them ideal for certifying ownership of digital art, collectibles, and other one-of-a-kind items. The ability to mint and trade NFTs on Stellar provides artists and creators with new revenue streams and a global audience. Furthermore, the low transaction fees and fast processing times associated with Stellar make it an attractive platform for both existing and emerging NFT marketplaces.

Security and scalability are critical considerations in the context of tokenization. The Stellar network employs robust security measures, ensuring that tokenized assets are protected from fraud and unauthorized access. Additionally, Stellar's architecture is designed to handle high transaction volumes efficiently, making it suitable for widespread adoption in various sectors. As tokenization continues to evolve, its integration with philanthropy and humanitarian aid projects will also become more prominent, enabling transparent and accountable donations that can be tracked on the blockchain. This potential for social impact underscores the transformative power of tokenization within the broader landscape of cryptocurrencies and financial innovation.

Benefits of Asset Tokenization

Asset tokenization offers a range of benefits that can significantly enhance the efficiency and accessibility of various financial transactions. By converting physical or digital assets into tokens on the Stellar network, individuals and organizations can facilitate faster and more secure transactions across borders. This process not only streamlines traditional asset management but also reduces the time and costs associated with cross-border payments. With Stellar Lumens (XLM) serving as the backbone, asset tokenization allows for real-time transactions, eliminating delays that typically occur in conventional banking systems.

One of the most compelling advantages of asset tokenization is enhanced liquidity. Tokenized assets can be traded on decentralized exchanges, providing investors with greater opportunities to buy and sell their holdings. This increased liquidity makes it easier for asset owners to convert their investments into cash when needed, thereby improving their overall financial flexibility. Additionally, the ability to fractionalize assets allows a broader range of investors to participate in markets that were previously inaccessible, such as real estate or fine art, democratizing investment opportunities.

Tokenization on the Stellar network also enhances transparency and traceability. Each transaction involving a token is recorded on the blockchain, creating an immutable ledger that can be audited by all parties involved. This transparency mitigates the risks of fraud and enhances trust between participants in a transaction. Investors can verify the authenticity and ownership of tokenized assets without relying on intermediaries, fostering a more efficient and secure investment environment. The use of smart contracts further automates these processes, ensuring that all parties fulfill their obligations without the need for manual intervention.

Moreover, asset tokenization supports regulatory compliance more effectively than traditional methods. The programmable nature of tokens allows issuers to embed compliance protocols directly into the token's smart contract. This ensures that transactions adhere to local regulations, such as KYC (Know Your Customer) and AML (Anti-Money Laundering) requirements, reducing the burden on businesses and enhancing the legitimacy of transactions. As regulatory scrutiny increases in the cryptocurrency space, this feature of asset tokenization is crucial for fostering trust among investors and institutions alike.

Finally, the impact of asset tokenization extends beyond individual investors to broader economic implications. By improving access to capital and liquidity, tokenized assets can stimulate investment in various sectors, including real estate, infrastructure, and innovation. In humanitarian contexts, tokenization can streamline the flow of charitable donations, ensuring that funds are distributed efficiently and transparently. The potential for tokenized assets to empower economic growth and facilitate philanthropic efforts highlights the transformative power of this technology within the Stellar ecosystem.

Examples of Tokenized Assets on Stellar

Tokenized assets on the Stellar network represent a significant advancement in the way we view and manage ownership of various assets. Stellar enables the creation of digital representations of real-world assets, allowing them to be easily traded, transferred, and utilized within a decentralized framework. This tokenization process simplifies transactions and enhances liquidity, making it particularly appealing for cross-border payments and decentralized finance (DeFi) applications. By leveraging Stellar's platform, businesses and individuals can engage in the global economy with greater efficiency and less friction.

One prominent example of tokenized assets on Stellar is the tokenization of fiat currencies. Companies have developed stablecoins that are pegged to traditional currencies, allowing users to transact in a digital format while maintaining stability in value. For instance, a USD-pegged stablecoin on Stellar facilitates cross-border payments without the volatility typically associated with cryptocurrencies. This enables individuals and businesses to send and receive money internationally in a manner that resembles traditional banking transactions, yet operates on a decentralized network that is faster and more cost-effective.

In addition to fiat currencies, Stellar has become a platform for tokenizing physical assets, such as real estate and commodities. By representing these assets as tokens on the blockchain, owners can fractionalize their investments, making high-value assets more accessible to a broader range of investors. This democratization of investment opportunities not only enhances liquidity but also allows for innovative financing solutions. For example, a real estate company can issue tokens representing shares in a property, enabling multiple investors to own a stake without the need for complex legal arrangements or extensive paperwork.

Another fascinating application of tokenization on Stellar is the creation of non-fungible tokens (NFTs). While NFTs are often associated with digital art and collectibles, the Stellar network enables the tokenization of unique assets across various domains, including music, gaming, and intellectual property. This functionality allows creators to maintain ownership and control over their work while providing a secure and transparent marketplace for buyers. The low transaction costs and fast processing times on Stellar further enhance the appeal of NFTs, making it easier for artists and developers to monetize their unique creations.

Smart contracts play a crucial role in the automation of processes related to tokenized assets on the Stellar network. By enabling self-executing agreements, smart contracts can streamline transactions, ensuring that terms are fulfilled without the need for intermediaries. This capability is particularly beneficial in DeFi applications, where users can engage in lending, borrowing, and trading in a trustless environment. As tokenized assets continue to evolve on Stellar, the integration of smart contracts will further enhance the functionality and efficiency of cross-border payments and other financial services, solidifying Stellar's position as a leading player in the cryptocurrency space.

Chapter 7: Smart Contracts and Automation in Stellar

Introduction to Smart Contracts

Smart contracts represent a transformative innovation in the realm of blockchain technology, particularly within the Stellar network. At their core, smart contracts are self-executing contracts with the terms of the agreement directly written into code. This automation reduces the need for intermediaries, streamlining processes and enhancing efficiency. As businesses and individuals increasingly seek solutions for cross-border payments, the ability to execute complex agreements automatically and transparently becomes crucial. With Stellar Lumens facilitating fast and low-cost transactions, smart contracts can significantly improve the speed and reliability of international financial agreements.

The integration of smart contracts into cross-border payment systems can address long-standing challenges such as high fees, lengthy processing times, and the inherent risk of fraud. By utilizing Stellar's decentralized infrastructure, smart contracts can facilitate transactions that are not only faster but also more secure. For example, a smart contract can be programmed to release funds automatically once certain conditions are met, ensuring that both parties fulfill their obligations. This level of trust and reliability is particularly important in international trade, where parties may be hesitant to engage without established systems in place.

In the context of decentralized finance (DeFi) applications on Stellar, smart contracts unlock a plethora of opportunities for innovation. They enable the creation of decentralized lending and borrowing platforms, allowing users to engage in peer-to-peer transactions without relying on traditional financial institutions. This democratization of finance can empower individuals in developing regions, where access to banking services is limited. By leveraging smart contracts, DeFi projects can operate efficiently on the Stellar network, providing users with a seamless experience while maintaining security and transparency.

Moreover, the use of smart contracts extends beyond financial transactions to include the tokenization of assets and non-fungible tokens (NFTs). Smart contracts can govern the creation and transfer of digital assets on the Stellar network, simplifying the process of asset management and ownership transfer. This capability is particularly relevant for artists and creators in the NFT space, who can utilize smart contracts to establish provenance and automate royalty payments. As the NFT market continues to grow, the role of smart contracts in ensuring fair and transparent transactions will be increasingly vital.

Lastly, the security and scalability of the Stellar network enhance the effectiveness of smart contracts. The architecture of Stellar is designed to handle a high volume of transactions while maintaining robust security measures, making it an ideal platform for deploying smart contracts. As the demand for innovative solutions in philanthropy and humanitarian aid projects rises, smart contracts can ensure that funds are allocated efficiently and transparently. By automating compliance and reporting processes, organizations can focus more on their mission and less on administrative burdens, thereby maximizing their impact on the ground.

How Smart Contracts Work on Stellar

Smart contracts on the Stellar network revolutionize the way transactions and agreements are executed by automating processes through self-executing code. Unlike traditional contracts, which require intermediaries to enforce the terms, smart contracts on Stellar leverage the network's decentralized infrastructure to ensure that agreements are enforced without human intervention. This automation significantly reduces the chances of disputes and enhances the efficiency of cross-border payments, making it an attractive option for businesses and individuals alike.

The Stellar network utilizes a unique approach to smart contracts, focusing on simplicity and speed. Instead of deploying complex code, Stellar smart contracts often utilize multi-signature accounts and transaction batching to create conditional transactions. This method allows for the execution of contracts based on predefined criteria, such as the completion of payment or the verification of identity. By keeping the smart contract functionality lightweight, Stellar maintains fast transaction speeds, which are critical for applications in the fast-paced world of cross-border payments and financial transactions.

In addition to facilitating payments, Stellar smart contracts play a crucial role in decentralized finance (DeFi) applications. These contracts enable the creation of decentralized exchanges, lending platforms, and other financial services that operate without central authorities. By providing a secure and transparent environment, Stellar's smart contracts foster trust among users, thereby encouraging the adoption of DeFi solutions. Investors can benefit from these applications by participating in liquidity pools or earning yields on their investments, all while enjoying the security and efficiency that Stellar offers.

The utility of smart contracts extends to the realm of non-fungible tokens (NFTs) and asset tokenization on the Stellar network. Creators can use smart contracts to define the ownership, transfer, and royalties associated with their digital assets. This capability not only enhances the value proposition of NFTs but also allows for fractional ownership of real-world assets. By tokenizing assets, Stellar opens up new avenues for investment and ownership, enabling individuals and institutions to diversify their portfolios and engage in innovative financial opportunities.

Security and scalability are paramount in the design of smart contracts on Stellar. The network employs a consensus mechanism that ensures transactions are validated quickly and securely, minimizing the risk of fraud or manipulation. Moreover, the ability to handle thousands of transactions per second positions Stellar as an ideal platform for high-volume applications. As organizations increasingly look to incorporate blockchain technology into their operations, the robust security and scalability of Stellar's smart contracts will be a key factor in driving their adoption for philanthropic initiatives and humanitarian aid projects, thereby enhancing their impact on global challenges.

Applications of Smart Contracts in Cross-Border Payments

Smart contracts have emerged as a transformative technology within the realm of cross-border payments, particularly when integrated with blockchain networks like Stellar. These self-executing contracts, coded with the terms of an agreement directly into the software, offer unprecedented efficiency and security for international transactions. By eliminating intermediaries, smart contracts facilitate direct interactions between parties, reducing transaction times from days to mere seconds, which is crucial in global finance where delays can impact business operations and financial liquidity.

One of the most significant applications of smart contracts in cross-border payments is their ability to automate compliance with regulatory requirements. Each transaction can be programmed to automatically adhere to the rules of the involved jurisdictions, ensuring that all necessary checks—such as anti-money laundering (AML) and know-your-customer (KYC) protocols—are executed without manual intervention. This not only enhances the reliability of transactions but also minimizes the risk of legal repercussions for businesses operating across multiple regulatory environments.

Moreover, smart contracts enhance transparency in cross-border payments. All actions taken within a smart contract are recorded on a public ledger, enabling all parties involved to trace the transaction history and verify the integrity of the payment. This transparency fosters trust among participants, particularly in regions where traditional banking systems may be less reliable or where fraud is a significant concern. As a result, organizations can operate with greater confidence, knowing that their transactions are secure and verifiable.

In addition to compliance and transparency, smart contracts can also facilitate complex payment structures that are often required in international trade. For example, businesses can set up multi-signature requirements, where payments are released only when specific conditions are met, such as the delivery of goods or the completion of services. This conditional payment structure not only protects the interests of both buyers and sellers but also reduces the potential for disputes, ensuring smoother transactions across borders.

Finally, the integration of smart contracts with Stellar's decentralized finance (DeFi) infrastructure opens up new avenues for financial inclusion. By enabling low-cost, efficient cross-border payments, smart contracts can empower individuals and businesses in developing regions, where access to traditional banking services is limited. This democratization of financial services can drive economic growth and enhance the capabilities of local enterprises, ultimately contributing to a more equitable global financial landscape. As the adoption of Stellar Lumens and its smart contract functionality continues to grow, we can expect to see even more innovative applications that will reshape the future of cross-border payments.

Chapter 8: Stellar Network Security and Scalability

Security Features of the Stellar Network

The Stellar Network incorporates several security features designed to protect transactions and user assets while maintaining a decentralized and efficient framework. At its core, Stellar utilizes a consensus mechanism known as the Stellar Consensus Protocol (SCP). Unlike traditional proof-of-work systems, SCP relies on a federated Byzantine agreement model that allows nodes to reach consensus without the need for a central authority. This decentralized approach minimizes the risk of single points of failure and enhances the overall resilience of the network against malicious attacks.

Stellar also employs cryptographic techniques to secure user identities and transaction data. Each user on the network possesses a unique public-private key pair, ensuring that only the rightful owner can authorize transactions. This cryptographic security layer not only protects against unauthorized access but also ensures the integrity of data being exchanged. Furthermore, all transactions on the Stellar Network are recorded on a public ledger, enhancing transparency and providing a verifiable audit trail for all network activities.

Another critical aspect of Stellar's security architecture is its built-in anti-fraud mechanisms. The network allows users to set trust lines, enabling them to specify which assets they are willing to accept from other accounts. This feature helps prevent fraudulent transactions by ensuring that assets can only be transferred between trusted parties. Additionally, the Stellar Development Foundation continuously monitors the network for unusual activities and implements upgrades and patches to address any vulnerabilities that may arise.

The scalability of the Stellar Network also contributes to its security. By efficiently processing thousands of transactions per second, Stellar mitigates the risk of network congestion, which can lead to delays and potential vulnerabilities. This high throughput, combined with the network's ability to handle large volumes of transactions, ensures that the system remains robust even during peak usage periods. As a result, investors and users can engage in cross-border payments with confidence, knowing that their transactions are secure and processed swiftly.

In summary, the security features of the Stellar Network are integral to its functionality and appeal in the realms of cross-border payments and decentralized finance. By leveraging advanced consensus protocols, cryptographic safeguards, anti-fraud measures, and scalability solutions, Stellar provides a secure environment for users and investors alike. As the network continues to evolve, ongoing enhancements to its security framework will further solidify its position as a leading platform for financial transactions and innovative applications such as NFTs and smart contracts.

Addressing Scalability Challenges

Addressing scalability challenges is crucial for the widespread adoption of the Stellar network, especially as the demand for cross-border payments and decentralized finance applications continues to grow. Scalability refers to the network's ability to handle an increasing number of transactions efficiently without compromising speed or security. As more users and applications are built on Stellar, the network must ensure that it can scale effectively to accommodate this growth while maintaining its core principles of decentralization and low transaction costs.

One of the primary scalability solutions employed by Stellar is its unique consensus mechanism, the Stellar Consensus Protocol (SCP). Unlike traditional proof-of-work systems, which can become bogged down by the sheer volume of transactions, SCP allows for rapid transaction confirmation through its federated Byzantine agreement model. This model enables nodes to reach consensus without requiring every participant to validate every transaction, leading to faster processing times and a higher throughput of transactions per second. This innovative approach helps Stellar maintain a competitive edge in the realm of cross-border payments.

In addition to its consensus mechanism, Stellar is also designed to facilitate interoperability with other blockchain networks and financial systems. The ability to connect with various platforms allows Stellar to integrate additional scalability solutions, such as layer-two protocols or sidechains, which can offload some transaction volume from the main network. This flexibility is particularly beneficial for decentralized finance applications that may require different transaction speeds and costs depending on user needs. By embracing interoperability, the Stellar network can adapt and scale to meet the demands of an evolving financial landscape.

Tokenization of assets on the Stellar network also contributes to addressing scalability challenges. By allowing real-world assets to be represented as digital tokens, Stellar can streamline processes such as cross-border transactions and asset transfers. This tokenization not only enhances liquidity but also reduces the complexity of conducting transactions involving multiple currencies and regulatory environments. As more assets are tokenized and traded on the network, the increased volume can drive further innovation and efficiency, reinforcing Stellar's position in the decentralized finance ecosystem.

Finally, the implementation of smart contracts and automation within the Stellar network plays a pivotal role in enhancing scalability. Smart contracts enable developers to create self-executing agreements that can facilitate complex transactions without requiring constant human intervention. This automation reduces the time and resources needed to process transactions, allowing the network to handle more simultaneous operations. As the adoption of smart contracts grows, so too will the capacity of the Stellar network to support a diverse range of applications, from NFTs to philanthropic initiatives, ultimately addressing scalability challenges while fostering a vibrant ecosystem.

Future Developments in Stellar Security and Scalability

The future developments in stellar security and scalability are critical to the ongoing evolution of the Stellar network. As cross-border payments become increasingly vital in a globalized economy, the need for robust security measures is paramount. Innovations such as advanced cryptographic techniques will play a significant role in safeguarding transactions. The Stellar Development Foundation is likely to implement state-of-the-art security protocols to protect users from fraud and unauthorized access. This focus on security is essential not only for individual users but also for institutions looking to adopt Stellar for their financial operations.

Scalability is another fundamental aspect of Stellar's future, particularly as the volume of transactions increases with wider adoption. The network currently boasts impressive transaction speeds and low costs, but further enhancements are expected. Future developments may include the implementation of sharding and other scaling solutions that allow the network to process millions of transactions per second without compromising performance. This scalability will be vital for accommodating the growing number of decentralized finance (DeFi) applications and non-fungible tokens (NFTs) built on Stellar, ensuring smooth operations even during peak usage times.

In the realm of decentralized finance, the integration of smart contracts is set to revolutionize the Stellar network. These self-executing contracts will automate complex financial transactions, ranging from lending to asset management. Future developments may introduce user-friendly tools for developers, allowing them to create and deploy smart contracts seamlessly. As more DeFi applications emerge on the Stellar platform, the demand for reliable and efficient smart contract functionality will drive the network's evolution, making it an attractive option for investors and developers alike.

Tokenization of assets is another area ripe for future enhancement. By enabling the digitization of real-world assets, Stellar can facilitate easier trading and transfer of ownership. Future advancements may see the introduction of more sophisticated token standards and regulatory compliance measures, making it simpler for businesses and individuals to tokenize a variety of assets. This capability will not only widen the scope of investment opportunities but will also foster greater liquidity in markets that have traditionally been illiquid, thus appealing to a broader audience of investors.

Finally, the role of Stellar in philanthropy and humanitarian aid projects underscores the importance of continuous improvement in security and scalability. As organizations increasingly leverage blockchain technology for transparency and efficiency in funding distribution, Stellar's future developments will be crucial. Enhanced security mechanisms will help ensure that funds are allocated appropriately, while scalable solutions will allow for rapid disbursement of aid to those in need. By focusing on these areas, Stellar can establish itself as a leading platform for social impact, attracting attention from both investors and nonprofits committed to making a difference in the world.

Chapter 9: The Role of XLM in Philanthropy and Humanitarian Aid Projects

Overview of Philanthropy in the Crypto Space

Philanthropy in the crypto space has emerged as a transformative force, leveraging blockchain technology to enhance the efficiency and transparency of charitable giving. This sector has witnessed a surge in interest as cryptocurrencies like Stellar Lumens (XLM) provide mechanisms to facilitate cross-border donations with minimal fees and instant transaction times. The decentralized nature of blockchain eliminates intermediaries, allowing donors to contribute directly to causes they support, thereby fostering a more direct connection between contributors and recipients. This shift not only enhances trust in philanthropic initiatives but also attracts a new generation of donors who are more inclined to use digital currencies for their charitable activities.

Numerous organizations have begun to embrace cryptocurrencies, recognizing their potential to streamline operations and broaden their reach. By adopting Stellar Lumens, these organizations can raise funds from a global audience without the constraints imposed by traditional banking systems. For instance, the ability to convert various fiat currencies into XLM seamlessly allows charities to operate internationally, collecting donations from diverse sources while minimizing currency conversion fees. This capability is particularly beneficial for humanitarian efforts that require swift response to crises, where timely funds can significantly impact those in need.

In addition to facilitating donations, the Stellar network offers innovative solutions for tracking the flow of funds. Smart contracts can automate the distribution of donations, ensuring that funds are released only when specific conditions are met, thus increasing accountability. This feature addresses one of the major concerns in philanthropy: the misuse of funds. By utilizing blockchain's immutable ledger, organizations can provide real-time updates on how donations are being utilized, enhancing transparency and fostering greater trust among donors. The use of this technology not only improves the efficacy of charitable initiatives but also encourages more individuals to engage in philanthropy through cryptocurrencies.

Philanthropy on the Stellar network is also witnessing the rise of Non-Fungible Tokens (NFTs) as a new fundraising tool. Artists and creators are leveraging NFTs to generate revenue for charitable causes, with a portion of sales directed toward specific projects. This intersection of art and philanthropy allows for unique and engaging ways to raise funds while simultaneously promoting awareness of various issues. Furthermore, the tokenization of assets can enable fractional ownership of high-value items, where proceeds from sales can benefit charitable organizations, creating a novel avenue for fundraising that aligns with the preferences of digital-savvy investors.

As the landscape of philanthropy in the crypto space continues to evolve, it is evident that Stellar Lumens plays a pivotal role in shaping these initiatives. The combination of low transaction fees, scalability, and security offered by the Stellar network empowers organizations to innovate in their fundraising strategies. As more charitable entities adopt these technologies, the potential for impactful giving increases, paving the way for a future where cryptocurrency philanthropy becomes a standard practice. By understanding the synergies between blockchain technology and philanthropy, investors and individuals alike can contribute to a more equitable and responsive global community.

Notable Humanitarian Projects Using XLM

Notable humanitarian projects utilizing Stellar Lumens (XLM) have emerged as significant examples of how blockchain technology can address global challenges. These projects leverage the speed and low transaction costs of the Stellar Network to facilitate cross-border payments, thereby enhancing access to financial resources for underserved populations. By enabling efficient transactions, these initiatives aim to improve the lives of those in need, demonstrating the practical applications of XLM beyond traditional financial systems.

One prominent example is the partnership between Stellar and the United Nations' World Food Programme (WFP). This collaboration aims to provide cash assistance to vulnerable communities facing food insecurity. By using XLM, the WFP can quickly and transparently distribute funds to beneficiaries in regions affected by conflict or natural disasters. The use of blockchain technology allows for real-time tracking of funds, ensuring that aid reaches its intended recipients without the delays often associated with conventional banking systems.

Another noteworthy project is the collaboration between Stellar and various non-governmental organizations (NGOs) working in refugee assistance. These organizations have adopted the Stellar Network to create digital wallets for refugees, enabling them to receive, store, and transfer funds securely. This approach not only empowers refugees by providing them with financial independence but also reduces the risks associated with carrying cash in unstable environments. The low transaction fees associated with XLM make it an attractive option for NGOs that often operate with tight budgets.

In addition to cash assistance, projects focused on healthcare access are also making significant strides with Stellar Lumens. For instance, initiatives that utilize XLM to streamline payment processes for medical services in remote areas are gaining traction. By reducing the friction in cross-border payments, healthcare providers can receive payments faster, allowing them to offer essential services without interruption. This is particularly crucial in regions where traditional banking infrastructure is lacking, ensuring that individuals can access necessary medical care without financial barriers.

Lastly, the role of XLM in supporting educational initiatives cannot be overlooked. Various projects have emerged that use Stellar to facilitate micro-donations for educational programs in developing countries. By enabling direct and transparent funding from donors to educational institutions, these initiatives help improve access to quality education. The ability to track donations on the Stellar Network ensures accountability and encourages more people to contribute, fostering a culture of support for education in underserved communities. Through these diverse applications, XLM is proving to be a powerful tool for humanitarian aid and development, showcasing the transformative potential of blockchain technology.

The Impact of Stellar on Global Philanthropy

The impact of Stellar on global philanthropy is profound, as it introduces a new paradigm for how charitable contributions are made and distributed. Traditional philanthropy often faces challenges such as high transaction fees, slow processing times, and a lack of transparency. Stellar Lumens, with its robust blockchain technology, offers a solution by enabling near-instant transactions at a fraction of the cost. This efficiency allows organizations to allocate more resources directly to the causes they support, maximizing the impact of donations and helping to ensure that funds reach those in need more quickly.

One of the key advantages of using Stellar in philanthropy is its capacity for cross-border payments. Many charitable organizations operate in multiple countries, and transferring funds across borders can be fraught with delays and high fees. Stellar's decentralized network facilitates seamless transactions between different currencies, allowing organizations to bypass traditional banking hurdles. This capability is particularly crucial for humanitarian aid projects that require immediate funding in crisis situations, where time is of the essence and every second counts.

Moreover, Stellar enhances transparency and accountability in charitable giving. With its blockchain technology, each transaction is recorded on a public ledger that can be accessed by anyone. This feature allows donors to track where their contributions are going and how they are being used. Organizations can provide real-time updates on the allocation of funds, fostering trust and encouraging more individuals to contribute. By ensuring that financial flows are visible and verifiable, Stellar helps to combat fraud and mismanagement in the philanthropic sector.

The integration of smart contracts on the Stellar network further amplifies its impact on philanthropy. Smart contracts can automate the distribution of funds based on predefined conditions, ensuring that donations are released only when specific criteria are met. This functionality is particularly useful for projects that require milestone-based funding, as it aligns the interests of donors with the successful execution of humanitarian initiatives. By automating these processes, Stellar minimizes administrative overhead and enables organizations to focus more on their mission rather than on bureaucratic logistics.

Lastly, the tokenization of assets on the Stellar network opens new avenues for fundraising. Charitable organizations can create tokens representing various assets, such as real estate or artwork, and sell them to raise funds for specific projects. This innovative approach not only diversifies funding sources but also allows donors to engage with philanthropy in novel ways, potentially increasing overall contributions. As Stellar continues to evolve and integrate with decentralized finance (DeFi) applications, its role in global philanthropy is poised to expand, offering new tools and opportunities for impact-driven organizations and their supporters.

Chapter 10: The Future of Cross-Border Payments with Stellar

Trends Shaping the Future of Payments

The payments landscape is undergoing a significant transformation driven by several emerging trends that are reshaping how individuals and businesses transact across borders. One of the most notable trends is the increasing adoption of cryptocurrencies, particularly Stellar Lumens (XLM), as a viable alternative to traditional payment systems. As more people recognize the benefits of using digital currencies for cross-border transactions, the barriers associated with currency conversion, high fees, and lengthy processing times are beginning to diminish. The Stellar network, designed to facilitate fast and low-cost transactions, stands at the forefront of this shift, providing a robust platform for users to send and receive money globally.

Decentralized Finance (DeFi) applications are also playing a pivotal role in the future of payments. By leveraging the capabilities of the Stellar network, these applications offer users innovative financial solutions such as lending, borrowing, and yield farming without the need for intermediaries. As more investors and consumers become familiar with DeFi, the demand for seamless, decentralized payment solutions is likely to grow. Stellar's infrastructure supports the development of these applications, allowing developers to create user-friendly platforms that empower individuals to manage their finances more effectively, further catalyzing the adoption of digital currencies.

Another trend shaping the future of payments is the rise of tokenization, which involves converting physical assets into digital tokens on the blockchain. This process enables the fractional ownership of assets, making investments more accessible to a broader audience. Stellar's capabilities in tokenization allow for the creation of a wide range of asset-backed tokens, from real estate to art. As more investors recognize the advantages of tokenizing assets, the potential for cross-border transactions and investments will increase, further bolstering the utilization of Stellar Lumens as a medium of exchange in this evolving market.

Smart contracts are revolutionizing payment systems by automating agreements and transactions through self-executing contracts coded on the blockchain. In the context of the Stellar network, smart contracts can streamline payment processes, reduce fraud, and enhance transparency. As businesses and individuals seek greater efficiency in their financial dealings, the integration of smart contracts into payment solutions will become increasingly important. This technological advancement not only improves transaction speed but also builds trust among parties, fostering a more secure environment for cross-border payments and financial interactions.

Finally, the increasing emphasis on security and scalability within payment systems cannot be overlooked. As the number of users and transactions on networks like Stellar continues to grow, ensuring robust security measures and the ability to scale effectively is crucial. Stellar's consensus mechanism and network architecture are designed to handle high volumes of transactions securely, making it an attractive option for businesses and individuals alike. Furthermore, the application of XLM in philanthropic and humanitarian aid projects highlights the network's versatility in facilitating donations and support across borders, showcasing how the future of payments is not only about efficiency but also about making a positive impact on global communities.

The Potential of Stellar in Global Financial Inclusion

The potential of Stellar in global financial inclusion is profound, addressing the barriers that millions face in accessing financial services. Traditional banking systems often exclude underserved populations due to location, identity verification issues, and high transaction costs. Stellar's decentralized network offers a solution by enabling low-cost, fast cross-border payments that can reach users in remote areas without the need for traditional banking infrastructure. This capability is particularly critical in developing regions, where access to financial services is limited, and where even small transactions can have a significant impact on individuals and communities.

Stellar Lumens (XLM) facilitates transactions in a way that significantly reduces fees and processing times compared to conventional methods. This efficiency empowers users to send and receive money across borders with minimal cost, encouraging economic participation. By leveraging Stellar's blockchain technology, individuals can engage in commerce, save, and invest without the traditional barriers that come with banking services. The ability to transact easily and affordably can enhance the financial stability of families and promote entrepreneurship, driving local economies forward.

Moreover, Stellar's infrastructure supports decentralized finance (DeFi) applications that can further enhance financial inclusion. These applications can offer services such as lending, borrowing, and yield farming to unbanked populations, which traditional financial institutions often overlook. With the ability to create smart contracts on the Stellar network, users can engage in automated financial transactions with trust and transparency. This innovation opens up new avenues for financial services that are accessible to anyone with an internet connection, fostering a more inclusive financial ecosystem.

The integration of non-fungible tokens (NFTs) and asset tokenization on the Stellar platform also presents unique opportunities for financial inclusion. By tokenizing assets, individuals can gain fractional ownership of resources such as real estate or art, which were previously unattainable for many. This democratization of asset ownership can create new revenue streams and investment opportunities for low-income individuals. Additionally, NFTs can represent digital identities or educational credentials, providing access to services that require verification and improving opportunities for employment and education.

Lastly, Stellar's approach to scalability and security ensures that as more users join the network, the system can handle increased demand without sacrificing performance. The emphasis on secure transactions mitigates risks associated with fraud and loss, which are critical concerns for new users entering the digital financial landscape. Furthermore, Stellar's potential in philanthropic efforts and humanitarian aid projects highlights its commitment to fostering financial inclusion worldwide. By providing a stable and efficient means of transferring funds for aid, Stellar can help ensure that resources reach those in need quickly and effectively, reinforcing its role as a catalyst for positive change in the global financial landscape.

Predictions for the Next Decade in Cross-Border Payments

The next decade in cross-border payments is poised for significant transformation, driven by advancements in technology and the increasing adoption of cryptocurrencies like Stellar Lumens (XLM). As traditional banking systems struggle with the speed and cost of international transactions, the demand for decentralized solutions will continue to rise. Stellar Lumens, with its focus on facilitating low-cost transactions across borders, is likely to play a pivotal role in shaping this landscape. Enhanced interoperability between Stellar and other blockchain networks will facilitate seamless transactions, making cross-border payments faster and more efficient.

Decentralized Finance (DeFi) applications on the Stellar network are expected to proliferate, unlocking new financial opportunities for users worldwide. With the growing interest in DeFi, Stellar's capabilities will enable users to access a range of financial services without the need for traditional intermediaries. This will include lending, borrowing, and yield farming, all streamlined through smart contracts. As more developers build on the Stellar platform, we can anticipate a surge in innovative DeFi solutions tailored for cross-border transactions, creating a more inclusive financial ecosystem.

Non-Fungible Tokens (NFTs) will also find a place in the cross-border payments arena over the next decade. As the market for digital collectibles and unique assets matures, Stellar's blockchain can facilitate the creation and transfer of NFTs, particularly in regions where traditional asset ownership is challenged. By tokenizing real-world assets like art, real estate, or even intellectual property on the Stellar network, users can engage in cross-border transactions with ease, enhancing liquidity and accessibility. This fusion of NFTs and cross-border payments will likely open new avenues for investment and commerce.

The tokenization of assets on the Stellar network will revolutionize how value is transferred across borders. By allowing users to tokenize various assets, including currencies, commodities, and even personal assets, Stellar will provide an efficient means for cross-border transactions. This capability will simplify the process of buying, selling, and trading assets globally, thereby increasing market participation. As regulations around tokenized assets become clearer, Stellar's infrastructure will be well-positioned to support these developments, fostering trust and compliance in cross-border exchanges.

Security and scalability will be critical considerations as cross-border payment systems evolve over the next decade. The Stellar network is designed to be secure, with built-in features that protect against fraud and ensure the integrity of transactions. As the volume of cross-border payments grows, scalability will become essential to maintain performance and user experience. Stellar's unique consensus mechanism and focus on efficiency will allow it to handle increased transaction loads without compromising security. Additionally, the integration of XLM in philanthropic and humanitarian aid projects will demonstrate the network's potential to facilitate transparent and efficient donations across borders, highlighting the social impact of cross-border payments powered by Stellar Lumens.

www.ingramcontent.com/pod-product-compliance
Lightning Source LLC
Chambersburg PA
CBHW070421230526
45471CB00006B/2915